INTRODUCTION

In a bustling corner of the digital realm, where creativity knows no bounds and innovation is the heartbeat, there exists a place where dreams become websites, and visions materialize into vibrant, interactive reality. Imagine a scenario where a budding artist, Sarah, finds herself on the brink of showcasing her portfolio to the world. She's an aspiring photographer, an artist at heart, and her camera lens has captured breathtaking moments, each one speaking its unique language.

Sarah envisions a website that will serve as her digital gallery, a platform where her artistry can resonate with the world. But here's the twist—Sarah isn't a coding expert; HTML and CSS are alien languages to her. She's a visionary, not a programmer. And this is where our story truly begins.

In the realm of website creation, Sarah's predicament is far from unique. The internet has become the canvas of the 21st century, but not everyone possesses the technical mastery to paint their digital masterpiece. This is where Wix enters the scene—a game-changer, a bridge between aspiration and realization, a symphony of pixels and creativity, and the subject of our journey.

Welcome to the world of Wix, where anyone, from artists like Sarah to entrepreneurs, bloggers, and small business owners, can sculpt their digital presence with unparalleled ease and grace. This book is your portal into this vibrant universe, a comprehensive guide that will empower you to harness the immense potential of Wix and craft your digital legacy.

Whether you're an individual seeking to establish an online identity, a small business aiming to flourish in the digital age, or an entrepreneur yearning to reach a global audience, the possibilities are boundless. In the pages that follow, we'll embark on a journey through the intricacies of Wix, demystifying its tools, unraveling its power, and illuminating its potential to transform your dreams into reality.

Together, we'll explore the art of website design, the science of SEO, the magic of e-commerce, and the simplicity of mobile optimization. You'll discover how to create and curate content that captivates, engage your audience, and leave a lasting digital footprint.

As we journey deeper into the Wix ecosystem, you'll uncover the secrets of effective website management, the joy of problem-solving, and the exhilaration of growth. By the time you've turned the final page of this book, you'll not only have a stunning website but also the knowledge and confidence to evolve and expand your digital presence.

So, dear reader, if you've ever dreamt of a website that stands as a testament to your creativity, ambition, or expertise, this book is your compass. The world of Wix awaits, and your digital adventure is about to begin. Let's embark on this transformative journey together and master the art of website creation with Wix.

CHAPTER 1:

Getting Started with Wix

Introduction To Wix's Website Builder

In the ever-evolving landscape of the digital world, having a captivating online presence is no longer a luxury; it's a necessity. Whether you're an aspiring entrepreneur, a seasoned business owner, an artist, or simply someone with a passion to share, the internet provides an unparalleled platform to showcase your talents, products, or ideas to a global audience. But here's the catch – you don't need to be a web development guru to do it.

Enter Wix, a transformative force in the realm of website building. Imagine a tool that empowers you to craft stunning, professional-grade websites with the ease of arranging puzzle pieces. Gone are the days of grappling with lines of code, complex software, and exorbitant development costs. Wix beckons you into a world where creativity knows no bounds, and where the power to build and design your own website is firmly in your hands.

At its core, Wix is a game-changing website builder that places the tools of web design directly at your fingertips. Whether you're an absolute beginner or a seasoned webmaster, Wix welcomes you with open arms.

Its intuitive drag-and-drop interface, combined with a treasure trove of templates and features, makes it accessible to all.

In this chapter, we will embark on a journey into the heart of Wix's website builder. We will explore its user-friendly interface, learn how to navigate its features, and unlock the potential to create a website that reflects your unique vision and purpose.

From choosing the right template to customizing layouts, colors, and fonts, we will unravel the secrets of crafting a website that not only looks exceptional but also functions seamlessly. Whether you're a business owner aiming to attract more customers, an artist eager to showcase your portfolio, or simply someone with a message to share, Wix has the tools to transform your digital aspirations into reality.

So, fasten your seatbelt and prepare to embark on a journey that will empower you to design, create, and manage your own website like never before. Welcome to the world of Wix's website builder, where the possibilities are as boundless as your imagination.

Creating a Wix account

Your journey into the world of Wix begins with a simple yet crucial step: creating a Wix account. This account is your key to unlocking the vast array of features and tools that Wix offers for building and managing your website. In this chapter, we'll guide you through the process of creating your Wix account, ensuring you have a solid foundation to start your digital adventure.

Why Create A Wix Account?

Before we delve into the how, let's address the why. A Wix account offers several benefits:

1. Access to Website Builder: With a Wix account, you gain access to Wix's powerful website builder, which allows you to design, customize, and publish your website.

2. Template Selection: You can choose from a wide range of templates tailored to different types of websites, making it easier to start your project.

3. Content Management: A Wix account allows you to manage your website's content, including text, images, videos, and more.

4. App Market: Access to the Wix App Market, where you can integrate various third-party apps and features into your website.

5. Domain and Hosting: You can register a custom domain through Wix or connect an existing domain. Plus, Wix hosts your website, ensuring it's accessible to the world.

6. Community and Support: Join a vibrant community of Wix users and access Wix's customer support resources.

Now, let's walk through the steps to create your Wix account:

Step 1: Visit the Wix Website

• Open your web browser and go to the Wix website at www.wix.com.

Step 2: Sign Up

• Click the "Sign Up" button located in the top right corner of the Wix homepage.

Step 3: Choose How to Sign Up

• You have two options for creating your account:

o Email: Enter your email address, create a password, and click "Sign Up."

o Social Media: Alternatively, you can sign up using your Facebook or Google account by clicking on the respective icons.

Step 4: Verify Your Email (if using email)

• If you choose to sign up with your email, Wix will send you a verification email. Go to your email inbox, find the verification email from Wix, and click the verification link to confirm your account.

Step 5: Complete Your Profile

• Once your account is verified, you'll be prompted to complete your profile. This includes providing some basic information about yourself and your website's purpose. Fill in the details and click "Continue."

Step 6: Choose a Plan

• Wix offers a variety of plans, including a free plan and premium plans with additional features. Select the plan that best suits your needs. You can start with the free plan and upgrade later if necessary.

Step 7: Start Building

> **Congratulations! Your Wix account is now created. You can start building your website by selecting a template, customizing it, and adding content.**

By completing these steps, you've laid the foundation for

your Wix-powered website. In the upcoming chapters, we'll delve deeper into the world of Wix, exploring how to design, customize, and optimize your website to achieve your specific goals and aspirations. Get ready to bring your digital dreams to life with Wix!

Navigating the Wix dashboard

Once you've created your Wix account and embarked on your journey to build an amazing website, the next step is to familiarize yourself with the Wix dashboard. The dashboard is your command center, where you'll manage your website's settings, content, and various aspects of your online presence. In this chapter, we'll guide you through the key elements and functions of the Wix dashboard, ensuring you can navigate it with ease.

Logging In:

1. To access the Wix dashboard, go to the Wix website (www.wix.com) and click "Sign In" in the top right corner.

2. Enter your login credentials (email and password) and click "Log In."

The Dashboard Overview: After logging in, you'll land on your Wix dashboard. Here's what you can expect to see:

1. My Sites: This section displays all the websites you've created or are currently working on. Click on a site's thumbnail to enter the site editor.

2. Create a New Site: If you want to start a new website project, you can click this button to access the website builder and choose a template.

3. Upgrade: Here, you can view the details of your current plan and explore options to upgrade to a premium plan if needed.

4. Domains: This section allows you to manage your domain names. You can register new domains, connect existing ones, and set your primary domain.

5. Mailboxes: If you've connected a domain with email hosting, you can manage your email accounts in this section.

6. Inbox: If you've enabled Wix Chat or Wix Forms, this is where you'll manage your messages and form submissions.

7. Subscriptions: View and manage any premium apps or services you've subscribed to.

8. Get More: (App Market) Explore and add third-party apps and extensions from the Wix App Market to enhance your website's functionality.

Managing Your Website: To navigate and manage your website using the Wix dashboard, follow these steps:

1. Select Your Website: Click on the thumbnail of the website you want to work on within the "My Sites" section. This will take you to the site editor.

2. Dashboard Sidebar: In the site editor, you'll find a sidebar on the left. Here, you can access various elements like pages, design settings, media, and more. Click on each option to open the respective settings.

3. Top Menu: At the top of the editor, you'll see a menu with options like "Save," "Preview," and "Publish." Use these options to save your work, preview your website, and make it live on the internet when you're ready.

4. Settings: Click the "Settings" button to access essential site settings, including general settings, SEO, domain management, and more.

5. Help Center: If you need assistance or have questions,

the "?" icon in the top right corner provides access to the Wix Help Center, where you can find tutorials, FAQs, and support resources.

As you explore the Wix dashboard and dive deeper into the site editor, you'll discover a wealth of tools and options to design, customize, and manage your website. Each element is designed to simplify the process of creating your online masterpiece, whether it's a personal blog, an e-commerce store, or a professional portfolio.

Understanding The Wix Editor Vs. Wix Adi

One of the first decisions you'll encounter when using Wix to create your website is whether to start with the Wix Editor or Wix ADI (Artificial Design Intelligence). Both options offer distinct advantages and cater to different needs, so it's essential to understand their differences before making a choice.

Wix Editor:

The Creative Playground

• Full Control: The Wix Editor is your digital canvas, giving you complete creative control over the design, layout, and functionality of your website. It's ideal for users who want to fine-tune every aspect of their site.

• Drag-and-Drop Interface: The Editor boasts a user-friendly drag-and-drop interface, allowing you to add and arrange elements (text, images, videos, forms, etc.) exactly where you want them on the page.

• Design Flexibility: With the Wix Editor, you can choose

from a vast library of templates, but you're not confined to their initial designs. You can customize every detail, from colors and fonts to spacing and alignment.

• Advanced Features: The Editor provides access to an extensive set of tools and features, including e-commerce capabilities, blogging, memberships, bookings, and more. This makes it suitable for a wide range of website types, from personal blogs to online stores.

• Learning Curve: While the Wix Editor offers the most flexibility, it may have a steeper learning curve, especially for users who are new to website design. However, Wix provides comprehensive resources and tutorials to assist you.

Wix ADI (Artificial Design Intelligence):

Your Personal Website Designer

• Simplicity: Wix ADI is designed for those who want a hassle-free, rapid website creation experience. It's perfect for beginners or individuals who prefer a more guided approach.

• Automated Design: ADI employs artificial intelligence to create a website for you based on your responses to a few questions about your preferences and needs. It generates a complete website layout, design, and initial content in minutes.

• Quick Start: With Wix ADI, you can have a basic website up and running almost instantly, making it an excellent choice if you need a web presence urgently.

• Limited Customization: While ADI is incredibly convenient, it offers less customization compared to the

Wix Editor. You can still make changes to your ADI-generated site, but you'll have fewer options for fine-tuning the design.

• Scalability: For some users, the simplicity of ADI may suffice for their current needs, but they might outgrow its capabilities as their website evolves. In such cases, it's possible to transition your ADI-created site to the Wix Editor for more extensive customization.

Choosing Between Wix Editor and Wix ADI:

The choice between the Wix Editor and Wix ADI boils down to your specific goals, preferences, and level of expertise:

• If you seek complete control, have a clear vision of your website's design, and are willing to invest more time in customization, the Wix Editor is the way to go.

• If you want a website quickly and don't want to get bogged down in design decisions, Wix ADI can get you started with minimal effort.

Remember that, regardless of your initial choice, Wix allows you to switch between the Editor and ADI at any time, ensuring your website can grow and adapt as your needs change. So, whether you opt for the creative playground of the Wix Editor or the rapid deployment of Wix ADI, you're on your way to building a fantastic website.

Choosing The Right Plan

Choosing the Right Wix Plan

Selecting the right Wix plan is a crucial decision in your

website-building journey. Wix offers a range of plans, each tailored to different needs and budgets. In this section, we'll explore the available plans and provide guidance on how to choose the one that best suits your requirements.

1. Free Plan:

• Ideal For: Beginners, personal projects, hobbyists, testing the platform.

• Key Features:

o Access to Wix's website builder.

o Wix-branded domain (e.g., yourusername.wixsite.com).

o Basic storage and bandwidth.

o Wix ads on your site.

• Considerations: The free plan is an excellent starting point, but it comes with limitations. It's not suitable for businesses or professional websites due to the Wix branding and limited resources.

2. Connect Domain:

• Ideal For: Small personal websites or individuals who want a custom domain.

• Key Features:

o Use your custom domain (if you have one).

o Removes Wix ads.

o Basic storage and bandwidth.

• Considerations: This plan is a step up from the free plan, allowing you to connect your custom domain. However, it still has limited resources and isn't recommended for business-critical websites.

3. Combo Plan:

• Ideal For: Personal websites, blogs, small businesses.

• Key Features:

o Use of a custom domain (free domain for the first year).

o No Wix ads.

o Increased storage and bandwidth.

o Access to the Wix Site Booster app (for SEO optimization).

• Considerations: The Combo plan is a popular choice for small businesses and individuals who want a more professional online presence. It provides essential features and resources.

4. Unlimited Plan:

• Ideal For: Growing businesses, entrepreneurs, freelancers.

• Key Features:

o Use of a custom domain (free domain for the first year).

o No Wix ads.

o Unlimited bandwidth.

o Increased storage.

o Access to the Wix Site Booster and Visitor Analytics apps.

• Considerations: This plan offers ample resources and is suitable for most small to medium-sized businesses. It removes limitations on bandwidth, allowing your website to handle more traffic.

5. Pro Plan:

• Ideal For: Advanced business websites, e-commerce stores, advanced bloggers.

• Key Features:

o Use of a custom domain (free domain for the first year).

o No Wix ads.

o Highest storage capacity.

o Priority customer support.

o Access to the Wix Site Booster, Visitor Analytics, and Professional Logo apps.

• Considerations: The Pro plan is designed for those who need more storage and advanced features. It's ideal for larger e-commerce sites and businesses with higher demands.

6. VIP Plan:

• Ideal For: High-traffic websites, established businesses, online stores.

• Key Features:

o Use of a custom domain (free domain for the first year).

o No Wix ads.

o Unlimited bandwidth.

o Highest storage capacity.

o VIP customer support.

o Access to Wix Site Booster, Visitor Analytics, Professional Logo, and Priority Response apps.

• Considerations: The VIP plan is the top-tier option, offering the most resources, VIP support, and advanced features. It's suitable for high-traffic websites and established businesses.

How to Choose:

1. Assess Your Needs: Consider your website's purpose, expected traffic, and features required. Start with your current needs and anticipate future growth.

2. Budget: Determine how much you're willing to invest in your website. Wix plans cover a range of price points, so choose one that aligns with your budget.

3. Custom Domain: If having a custom domain (e.g., www.yourdomain.com) is essential, ensure the plan you select supports this.

4. E-commerce: If you plan to sell products online, look for plans that offer e-commerce capabilities.

5. Additional Apps: Check if the plan includes apps or features you need, such as SEO tools, analytics, or support options.

6. Trial Period: Remember that Wix offers a 14-day money-back guarantee. You can try a premium plan risk-free during this period and upgrade or downgrade as needed.

CHAPTER 2:

*Choosing Your Website's
Purpose and Audience*

Defining Your Website's Goals And Objectives

Defining your website's goals and objectives is a crucial first step in the website creation process, and Wix provides a platform that can help you achieve these goals effectively. Here's a step-by-step guide on how to define your website's goals and objectives using Wix:

1. Understand Your Audience:

• Before diving into the technical aspects, it's essential to know your target audience. Who are they? What are their needs, preferences, and behaviors? Understanding your audience will help you tailor your website's goals to meet their expectations.

2. Identify Your Primary Goals:

• Start by determining the primary purpose of your website. Common goals include:

o Showcase Portfolio: If you're an artist or photographer, your goal may be to showcase your work.

o Sell Products: If you're an e-commerce business, your goal is likely to sell products.

o Inform and Educate: For blogs or informational websites, the goal could be to educate or inform your audience.

o Generate Leads: If you offer services, your goal may be to capture leads or inquiries.

o Build an Online Community: Some websites aim to build a community or engage users through forums or social features.

3. Set Specific Objectives:

• Once you've identified your primary goal, break it down into specific, measurable objectives. For example:

o "Increase monthly website traffic by 30% within six months."

o "Generate 100 new leads through contact forms each month."

o "Achieve $5,000 in monthly sales revenue within the first year."

4. Align with Your Brand:

• Ensure that your goals align with your brand's identity and values. Your website should reflect your brand's personality and resonate with your target audience.

5. Consider User Experience (UX):

• Factor in user experience when defining your goals. Your website should be easy to navigate, mobile-friendly, and visually appealing to enhance user engagement.

6. Leverage Wix Features:

• Wix offers various features and apps that can help you achieve your goals. Explore the Wix App Market to find tools like e-commerce integrations, contact forms, booking systems, and more.

7. Create a Content Strategy:

• Develop a content strategy that aligns with your goals and objectives. Plan what type of content you'll create, how often you'll update it, and how it will support your objectives.

8. Implement Analytics:

• Use Wix's built-in analytics tools or integrate with third-party analytics platforms to track your website's performance. Regularly monitor metrics related to your goals, such as traffic, conversion rates, and user engagement.

9. Test and Iterate:

• After launching your website, continually test and iterate. If your goals aren't being met, analyze the data and make necessary adjustments to improve your website's performance.

10. Seek Feedback:

• Encourage user feedback through surveys, comments, or contact forms. This can provide valuable insights into how well your website is meeting its objectives.

11. Stay Updated:

• Keep up to date with Wix's features and updates. New tools and enhancements may become available that can further support your goals.

12. Review and Adjust:

• Periodically review your website's goals and objectives. As your business or personal projects evolve, your website's purpose may change, and your goals should adapt accordingly.

Exploring The Wix Editor Interface

The Wix Editor is a powerful tool that empowers you to design and customize your website with ease. It offers a user-friendly interface with various elements and features that allow you to create a unique and professional web presence. Let's explore the key components of the Wix Editor interface:

1. Dashboard:

• When you log in to Wix and select your website, you'll be taken to the Wix Editor dashboard. Here, you'll find a menu on the left-hand side that provides access to essential settings and tools for your website.

2. Toolbar:

• At the top of the editor, you'll see a toolbar that includes options for saving your work, previewing your website, and publishing it. You can also undo and redo actions using these controls.

3. Site Structure:

• On the left side of the editor, you'll find the site structure. This section allows you to see and navigate through your website's pages. You can add, delete, and organize pages from here.

4. Main Canvas:

• The central part of the editor is your main canvas. This is where you'll see a visual representation of your website. You can click on elements to select and edit them.

5. Elements Panel:

• On the left-hand side, below the site structure, you'll find the Elements panel. This panel contains a wide range of elements and widgets that you can drag and drop onto your canvas to build your website. Elements include text, images, videos, buttons, forms, and more.

6. Design Tools:

• Above the main canvas, you'll see design tools. Here, you can customize the design of your website, including changing fonts, colors, and backgrounds. You can also access alignment and spacing options to ensure your content looks polished.

7. Pages Panel:

• On the left side of the editor, you'll find the Pages panel. This panel allows you to manage your website's pages, including adding new pages, setting the homepage, and organizing your site's navigation.

8. Background Menu:

• In the top toolbar, you'll find a background menu that allows you to customize the background of your site, including adding images, videos, or colors.

9. App Market:

• The App Market icon, located in the left sidebar, provides access to a wide range of third-party apps and widgets that you can integrate into your website to enhance its functionality. This includes e-commerce, marketing, social media, and more.

10. Settings Menu:

• In the left sidebar, you'll also find a Settings menu. This is where you can access various settings related to your website, including general settings, SEO settings, domain management, and more.

11. Help and Support:

• In the upper-right corner of the editor, you'll find a "?" icon that provides access to the Wix Help Center. Here, you can find tutorials, FAQs, and support resources to assist you as you work on your website.

12. Save and Publish:

• In the top toolbar, you'll find buttons for saving your work and publishing your website. Clicking "Save" will save your changes, while "Publish" will make your website live on the internet.

13. Mobile Editor:

• Wix offers a dedicated mobile editor that allows you to customize the mobile version of your website. You can switch between desktop and mobile views to ensure your site looks great on all devices.

Customizing The Layout, Colors, And Fonts

One of the key aspects of creating a visually appealing and unique website is customizing the layout, colors, and fonts. The Wix Editor offers a range of tools and options to help you achieve the design you desire. Here's how to customize these elements:

1. Layout Customization:

• Click on an Element: To customize the layout of a specific element, click on it in the main canvas. This could be a section, text box, image, or any other element.

• Drag and Resize: Many elements can be resized by clicking and dragging their edges or corners. You can also drag elements to reposition them on the page.

• Duplicate and Delete: Use the options in the toolbar to duplicate or delete elements.

• Alignment and Spacing: The top toolbar provides options for aligning elements horizontally and vertically. You can also set spacing and margins to control how elements are positioned relative to each other.

• Group and Ungroup: You can group related elements together and ungroup them when needed. This is useful for maintaining consistent layouts.

2. Colors Customization:

• Background Color: To change the background color of a section or the entire page, select the section or the page and click on the "Background" option in the top toolbar. Choose a color from the color palette or enter a custom color code.

• Element Colors: To change the color of text, buttons, or other elements, select the element and use the "Text Color" or "Fill Color" option in the top toolbar to pick a color.

• Global Colors: Wix allows you to define and save custom color palettes that you can use consistently across your website. This helps maintain a cohesive design.

3. Fonts Customization:

• Text Elements: To change the font of a text element, select the text and use the "Font" dropdown menu in the top toolbar to choose from a variety of font options. You can also adjust the font size, style (bold, italic), and alignment.

• Text Color: As mentioned earlier, you can customize the text color using the "Text Color" option.

• Global Fonts: Like global colors, you can define global font styles to maintain consistency throughout your website. This ensures that fonts match your brand and design preferences.

4. Themes and Templates:

• Wix offers a wide selection of themes and templates that come pre-designed with cohesive layouts, colors, and fonts. You can start with a template that aligns with your vision and customize it to suit your needs.

5. Mobile Optimization:

• Don't forget to optimize your layout, colors, and fonts for mobile devices. The Wix Editor allows you to adjust the mobile view separately, ensuring your website looks great on smartphones and tablets.

6. Preview Your Changes:

• Use the "Preview" button in the top toolbar to see how your website looks with the customizations you've made. This helps you fine-tune the design before publishing it.

Adding and organizing pages

Adding and organizing pages is a fundamental part of creating a well-structured website in the Wix Editor. Whether you're building a simple blog or a complex e-commerce site, here's how to add and organize pages effectively:

Adding Pages:

1. Access the Pages Panel: On the left side of the Wix Editor, you'll find the Pages panel. Click on it to open.

2. Add a New Page:

o To add a new page, click the "+ Add Page" button.

o Select the type of page you want to add from the options provided. Common types include:

- Standard Page: A blank page you can design from scratch.

- Blog: If you want to add a blog to your site.

- Store: For e-commerce purposes.

- Contact: To create a contact page.

- Gallery: For image galleries.

o Give your page a name and click "Done."

3. Page Settings:

o Click on the new page you've added in the Pages panel to access its settings. Here, you can configure SEO settings, permissions, and other page-specific options.

Organizing Pages:

1. Change Page Order:

o To change the order of pages in your navigation menu, click and drag a page to a new position in the Pages panel. The order in the panel reflects the order in the website's navigation menu.

2. Subpages:

o You can create subpages to organize content hierarchically. To do this, simply drag a page under another page in the Pages panel. This creates a dropdown menu in your site's navigation.

3. Hide Pages:

o If you want to temporarily hide a page from your site's navigation, click on the page in the Pages panel, go to "Settings," and toggle on the "Hide Page" option.

4. Rename Pages:

o Click on a page in the Pages panel, then click on its name to edit it. This is especially useful for ensuring your navigation menu is clear and concise.

5. Delete Pages:

o To delete a page, click on it in the Pages panel and then click the "Delete" button. Be cautious with this action, as it permanently removes the page and its content.

Important Tips:

• Keep your navigation menu organized and user-friendly. Clear, logical navigation helps visitors find what they're looking for quickly.

• Think about the hierarchy of your content. Use subpages to group related content together. For example, if you have a "Services" page, you could create subpages for each service you offer.

• Ensure that each page has a unique and descriptive title, as this contributes to better SEO and user experience.

• Regularly review and update your page organization as your website evolves.

• Don't forget to optimize the mobile view of your navigation menu, as it may appear differently on smaller screens.

By adding and organizing pages strategically, you can create a website that is easy to navigate, well-structured, and user-friendly, which enhances the overall user experience.

CHAPTER 3:

*Search Engine
Optimization (SEO)*

Understanding The Basics Of Seo

Search Engine Optimization (SEO) is crucial for ensuring that your Wix website ranks well in search engine results, making it easier for potential visitors to find your site. Wix provides a range of tools and features to help you optimize your site for search engines. Here are the basics of SEO using Wix:

1. Keyword Research:

• Start by identifying relevant keywords related to your website's content. These are the words and phrases that people might use when searching for information or products related to your site.

2. On-Page SEO:

• Page Titles: Use descriptive and keyword-rich titles for each page of your website. Edit the page title in the Page Settings to make it SEO-friendly.

• Meta Descriptions: Write concise and engaging meta descriptions for your pages. These should provide a brief summary of what each page is about and include keywords.

• Heading Tags: Use heading tags (H1, H2, H3, etc.) to structure your content. Include keywords in your headings to improve SEO.

• Image Alt Text: Add descriptive alt text to your images. This not only improves accessibility but also helps search engines understand your images.

• URL Structure: Create clean and descriptive URLs for your pages. Avoid long, convoluted URLs with random characters.

3. Content Creation:

• Create high-quality, valuable, and relevant content that addresses the needs and interests of your target audience. Regularly update your content to keep it fresh.

4. Mobile Optimization:

• Ensure that your website is mobile-friendly. Wix automatically generates mobile versions of your site, but it's essential to review and adjust the mobile design to provide an optimal user experience.

5. Website Speed:

• A fast-loading website is favored by search engines. Use Wix's optimization tools and consider optimizing images to improve page loading times.

6. Link Building:

• Internal Links: Create internal links between pages on your website to help users navigate and improve the flow of SEO value throughout your site.

• Backlinks: Encourage high-quality websites to link to your content. Natural backlinks from reputable sources can boost your site's authority.

7. Social Media Integration:

• Integrate social sharing buttons on your website to encourage visitors to share your content. Social signals can indirectly impact your SEO.

8. SEO Apps and Tools:

• Wix offers various SEO apps and tools that can help you improve your website's SEO. These may include apps for keyword optimization, site audits, and more.

9. Submit Sitemaps:

• Wix automatically generates a sitemap for your website. Submit this sitemap to search engines like Google and Bing through their respective webmaster tools.

10. Analytics:

• Use analytics tools to monitor your website's performance, track traffic, and identify areas for improvement. Wix offers its own analytics dashboard, or you can integrate third-party tools like Google Analytics.

11. Regular Monitoring and Updates:

• SEO is an ongoing process. Regularly monitor your website's SEO performance, make necessary adjustments, and stay informed about changes in search engine algorithms.

12. SEO Education:

• Familiarize yourself with SEO best practices by reading guides and tutorials. Stay up to date with industry news to adapt to evolving SEO trends.

Wix provides a user-friendly environment for implementing these SEO practices, and with dedication and effort, you can improve your website's search engine rankings and visibility. Keep in mind that SEO is a long-term strategy, and results may take time to become noticeable.

Writing Compelling And Seo-Friendly Content

Writing compelling and SEO-friendly content is essential for attracting both human readers and search engines to your website. Here are some tips to help you create content that is engaging, informative, and optimized for search engines like Google:

1. Understand Your Audience:

• Before you start writing, have a clear understanding of your target audience's needs, interests, and pain points. What questions are they asking, and what problems are they trying to solve?

2. Keyword Research:

• Identify relevant keywords related to your content's topic. Use tools like Google Keyword Planner, SEMrush, or Ahrefs to find keywords with decent search volume and low competition.

3. Create High-Quality Content:

• Quality matters. Write informative, well-researched, and valuable content that addresses your audience's questions or concerns. Avoid thin, low-quality content.

4. Engaging Headlines:

• Craft compelling headlines that grab readers' attention and accurately represent the content. Include your primary keyword if possible.

5. Organized Structure:

• Structure your content with headings (H1, H2, H3, etc.) to make it scannable and easy to read. Use headings to break up content into sections and subsections.

6. Keyword Placement:

• Place your target keywords naturally throughout your content. Use them in the title, headings, body text, and meta description.

7. Avoid Keyword Stuffing:

• Avoid overusing keywords unnaturally. Write for humans, not just search engines. Google penalizes keyword stuffing.

8. Informative Meta Descriptions:

• Craft compelling meta descriptions for your content. These short snippets appear in search engine results and should entice users to click on your link.

9. Internal Linking:

• Include relevant internal links to other pages on your website. This helps users navigate and provides additional context to search engines.

10. High-Quality External Links:

• When necessary, include external links to reputable sources that support your content. This can boost your content's credibility.

11. Image Optimization:

• If you use images, optimize them by adding descriptive alt text, compressing their size, and ensuring they are relevant to your content.

12. Mobile Optimization:

• Ensure your content is mobile-friendly, as an increasing number of users access websites on mobile devices.

13. User Engagement:

• Encourage user engagement through comments, social sharing buttons, and clear calls to action (CTAs).

14. Proofread and Edit:

• Always proofread your content for grammar and spelling errors. Well-edited content appears more professional and credible.

15. Content Length:

• Content length can vary, but in-depth, comprehensive articles tend to perform well in search results. Aim for at least 1,000 words for informative articles.

16. Regular Updates:

• Keep your content up to date. Google values fresh and relevant information.

17. Analyze and Improve:

• Use analytics tools to monitor how your content is performing. Pay attention to metrics like organic traffic, bounce rate, and time on page. Use this data to make improvements.

18. Share on Social Media:

• Promote your content on social media platforms to increase its visibility and reach a wider audience.

19. Use SEO Plugins (If Applicable):

• If you're using a content management system (CMS) like WordPress, consider using SEO plugins like Yoast SEO to help optimize your content.

Remember, the primary goal of SEO-friendly content is to provide value to your audience. When your content is informative, engaging, and well-optimized, it's more likely to rank well in search results and attract organic traffic to your website.

Utilizing Wix's Seo Tools

Wix offers a range of built-in SEO tools and features that can help you optimize your website for search engines like Google. Here's how to utilize Wix's SEO tools effectively:

1. Wix SEO Wiz:

• Wix provides an SEO Wiz tool, which is a step-by-step wizard that guides you through the process of optimizing your website for search engines. To access it:

o Go to your Wix dashboard.

o Click on "Marketing & SEO" in the left-hand menu.

o Select "SEO Tools."

o Click "Get Started" under "Wix SEO Wiz."

• Follow the prompts to set up your SEO preferences, including keywords, locations, and website goals. Wix will generate an SEO plan tailored to your website.

2. Meta Tags:

• Wix allows you to customize meta tags for each page on your website. This includes the page title and meta description, which appear in search engine results. To edit meta tags:

o Click on the page in the Wix Editor.

o Go to "Page SEO" in the Page Settings.

o Edit the title and description to include relevant keywords and accurately represent your page's content.

3. Header Code:

• You can add header code to your site, which can be useful for integrating third-party SEO tools or services, such as Google Analytics or Google Tag Manager. To add header code:

o Go to your Wix dashboard.

o Click on "Settings" and then "Advanced."

o Under "Site Integration," you can add code to the "Site Header Code" section.

4. SEO Patterns:

• Wix allows you to set SEO patterns for specific types of pages on your site, such as blog posts or product pages. These patterns automatically generate SEO information for new pages you create. To set SEO patterns:

o Go to your Wix dashboard.

o Click on "Marketing & SEO" in the left-hand menu.

o Select "SEO Patterns."

o Customize the patterns for different page types.

5. URL Structure:

• Wix enables you to customize the URL structure for each page. Ensure that your URLs are descriptive, include relevant keywords, and are easy for users to understand. To edit URLs:

o Click on the page in the Wix Editor.

o Go to "Page SEO" in the Page Settings.

o Edit the URL under "Page URL."

6. Site Verification:

· Wix simplifies the process of verifying your site with search engines like Google. You can verify your site directly through the Wix dashboard. This is important for accessing webmaster tools and gaining insights into your website's performance.

7. Mobile Optimization:

· Wix ensures that your website is mobile-friendly by generating a mobile version automatically. However, you should review and adjust the mobile design to provide an optimal user experience on smartphones and tablets.

8. Regular Updates:

· Keep your content and website up to date. Google values fresh and relevant information, so regularly add new content and make updates as needed.

9. Analytics Integration:

· Integrate Google Analytics or other analytics tools to track your website's performance. Wix offers an option to add your Google Analytics tracking ID easily.

10. Blog SEO:

· If you have a blog on your Wix website, pay attention to SEO best practices for your blog posts, including keyword optimization, meta tags, and high-quality content.

By utilizing these SEO tools and features in Wix, you can improve your website's search engine visibility and increase its chances of ranking well in search results. Remember that SEO is an ongoing process, and regularly monitoring and updating your website's SEO strategy is key to long-term success.

Strategies For Improving Search Engine Rankings

Improving search engine rankings requires a combination of strategies and ongoing efforts to enhance your website's visibility on search engine results pages (SERPs). Here are some effective strategies to boost your website's search engine rankings:

1. Keyword Research:

• Conduct thorough keyword research to identify relevant and high-traffic keywords and phrases in your niche. Use tools like Google Keyword Planner, SEMrush, or Ahrefs to find valuable keywords that align with your content.

2. High-Quality Content:

• Create high-quality, informative, and engaging content that addresses the needs and questions of your target audience. Well-written, valuable content is more likely to rank well.

3. On-Page SEO:

• Optimize each page of your website for on-page SEO factors, including:

o Using target keywords in titles, headings, and content.

o Crafting descriptive and compelling meta titles and meta descriptions.

o Adding alt text to images.

o Creating user-friendly and mobile-responsive designs.

4. Mobile Optimization:

• Ensure that your website is fully optimized for mobile devices. Google gives preference to mobile-friendly websites in its rankings.

5. Page Load Speed:

• Optimize your website's speed by compressing images, using efficient coding practices, and leveraging browser caching. A faster website provides a better user experience and is favored by search engines.

6. Backlink Building:

• Develop a strategy to acquire high-quality backlinks from reputable websites in your industry or niche. Natural and relevant backlinks can significantly improve your website's authority.

7. Internal Linking:

• Utilize internal links to connect related pages and create a logical website structure. Internal linking can help distribute link equity and improve navigation for users.

8. Technical SEO:

• Conduct technical SEO audits to identify and fix issues like broken links, duplicate content, and crawl errors. Ensure your website's XML sitemap is properly configured and submitted to search engines.

9. Secure Website (HTTPS):

• Secure your website with HTTPS encryption. Google gives preference to secure websites in its search results.

10. Social Signals:

• Promote your content on social media platforms to generate social signals. Although the direct impact of social signals on rankings is debated, social media can indirectly drive traffic and engagement.

11. Local SEO:

• If you have a local business, optimize your website for local search by creating a Google My Business profile, obtaining customer reviews, and using local keywords.

12. Content Updates:

• Regularly update and refresh your existing content. Google prefers up-to-date, relevant content.

13. User Experience (UX):

• Ensure a positive user experience on your website. Easy navigation, fast load times, and clear calls to action can reduce bounce rates and improve rankings.

14. Analytics and Monitoring:

• Use analytics tools like Google Analytics and Google Search Console to monitor your website's performance, track keyword rankings, and identify areas for improvement.

15. Guest Blogging:

• Contribute guest posts to authoritative websites in your

niche. This can help you build your brand and earn valuable backlinks.

16. E-A-T (Expertise, Authoritativeness, Trustworthiness):

• Focus on establishing and showcasing expertise, authoritativeness, and trustworthiness in your content. Google considers E-A-T when ranking content in some niches.

17. Voice Search Optimization:

• As voice search grows in popularity, optimize your content for voice search queries by providing concise, conversational answers.

Remember that SEO is an ongoing process, and it may take time to see significant improvements in rankings. Consistency and a well-rounded approach to these strategies will contribute to long-term success in improving search engine rankings.

CHAPTER 4:

Advanced Features and Functionality

Integrating Third-Party Apps From The Wix App Market

Integrating third-party apps from the Wix App Market is an excellent way to enhance the functionality and features of your Wix website. The Wix App Market offers a wide range of apps and widgets that can be easily integrated into your website. Here's how to do it:

1. Access the Wix App Market:

• Log in to your Wix account and open the website you want to edit.

• In the left-hand sidebar, click on "App Market." This will take you to the Wix App Market, where you can browse and search for available apps.

2. Browse and Search for Apps:

• Use the search bar or browse through categories to find the app you want to integrate. You can explore categories like E-commerce, Marketing, Social, and more.

3. Add the App to Your Website:

• When you've found the app you want to use, click on it to view more details.

• Click the "Add to Site" button. You may be prompted to choose which website in your account you want to add the app to if you have multiple websites.

4. Configure the App:

• Once the app is added to your website, you may need to configure its settings. Click on the app in the editor to access its settings and customize it according to your needs.

5. Publish Your Changes:

• After configuring the app, make sure to click "Publish" to save your changes and make the app live on your website.

6. Test the App:

• It's a good practice to thoroughly test the app to ensure it works as expected on your website. This includes checking for compatibility, functionality, and user experience.

7. Manage Your Apps:

• You can manage and view the apps integrated into your website by going back to the Wix editor. In the left-hand sidebar, click on "My Apps" to see a list of all the apps you've added.

8. Upgrade or Remove Apps:

• Some apps in the Wix App Market offer free versions with limited features, while others have premium versions with more capabilities. Depending on your needs, you may choose to upgrade to a premium version.

• If you decide to remove an app, you can do so from the "My Apps" section in the editor. Click on the app you want to remove, and you'll have the option to delete it.

9. Explore App-Specific Support:

• If you encounter any issues or have questions about a specific app, you can often find support, tutorials, and FAQs related to that app within the Wix App Market.

By integrating third-party apps from the Wix App Market, you can add features such as contact forms, e-commerce functionality, social media feeds, chat widgets, and more to your website, enhancing its overall functionality and user experience.

Setting Up An Online Store With Wix Ecommerce

Setting up an online store with Wix eCommerce is a straightforward process that allows you to sell products or services online. Here's a step-by-step guide to help you get started:

1. Sign in or Create a Wix Account:

• If you don't already have a Wix account, sign up for one. If you do, sign in to your account.

2. Choose a Template:

• After signing in, you can start by choosing a template for your online store. Wix offers various eCommerce templates designed specifically for online businesses. Select one that suits your business's style and needs.

3. Customize Your Template:

• Use the Wix Editor to customize your chosen template. You can modify the design, add your branding elements (logo, colors, fonts), and adjust the layout to fit your products or services.

4. Add Products:

• To add products to your online store, follow these steps:

o In the Wix Editor, click on "Add" in the left sidebar.

o Select "Store" and then click on "Add Products."

o Begin adding your products one by one, including product names, descriptions, prices, and images. You can also categorize products and add variants (e.g., different sizes or colors) if needed.

5. Set Up Payment Options:

• To enable customers to make purchases, you need to set up payment options. Wix eCommerce supports various payment gateways like PayPal, Stripe, and more. Follow these steps:

o In the Wix Editor, click on "Settings" and then select "Accept Payments."

o Choose the payment methods you want to offer and follow the setup instructions for each.

6. Configure Shipping:

• Set up shipping options and rates based on your location and the regions you plan to ship to. You can specify shipping costs, delivery times, and methods. To configure shipping:

o In the Wix Editor, go to "Settings" and select "Shipping & Pickup."

o Add your shipping zones, methods, and rates.

7. Add a Shopping Cart:

• Make sure your online store includes a shopping cart

feature that displays the items customers have added. Typically, this is automatically included in your Wix eCommerce template.

8. Set Up Taxes:

• If your business is required to charge taxes, configure the appropriate tax settings. Wix allows you to specify tax rates based on your location and customer location.

o In the Wix Editor, click on "Settings" and choose "Tax."

o Add the applicable tax rates and regions.

9. Configure Checkout Settings:

• Customize the checkout process to your liking. You can add checkout fields, enable guest checkout, and set up automated emails for order confirmations.

o In the Wix Editor, go to "Settings" and select "Checkout."

10. Test Your Online Store:

bash

- Before making your online store live, thoroughly test it. Make test purchases, review the checkout process, and ensure that everything works as expected.

11. Launch Your Online Store:

vbnet

- Once you are satisfied with your online store and have tested it, you can publish it to make it live on the internet.

12. Promote Your Online Store:

css

- Promote your online store through various channels,

including social media, email marketing, search engine optimization (SEO), and paid advertising, to attract customers and drive sales.

Wix provides a user-friendly platform for setting up and managing your online store. Regularly update your product listings, track sales and inventory, and continue optimizing your website to provide the best possible shopping experience for your customers.

Implementing Advanced Features

Implementing advanced features and functionalities like bookings, events, or memberships on your Wix website can greatly enhance its interactivity and usefulness. Here's how to add these advanced features to your Wix website:

1. Bookings:

• Wix offers the "Wix Bookings" app that allows you to set up a booking system for services or appointments.

• To add bookings to your website, follow these steps:

1. In the Wix Editor, click "Add" on the left sidebar.

2. Under "Apps," select "Bookings & Services."

3. Choose the "Wix Bookings" app and add it to your site.

4. Customize the settings, including the types of services you offer, availability, scheduling, and pricing.

5. Integrate payment options for booking fees if applicable.

6. Add a booking form or calendar to your website where users can book your services.

2. Events:

• To showcase and manage events on your Wix website,

follow these steps:

1. In the Wix Editor, click "Add" on the left sidebar.

2. Under "Apps," select "Events & Bookings."

3. Choose the "Wix Events" app and add it to your site.

4. Create event listings, including event titles, descriptions, dates, times, and locations.

5. Customize event registration and RSVP options.

6. Add event pages to your website where users can view and register for events.

7. Optionally, integrate a ticketing or payment system for paid events.

3. Memberships:

• To implement a membership system on your Wix website, you can use the "Wix Members" app:

1. In the Wix Editor, click "Add" on the left sidebar.

2. Under "Apps," select "Members & Login."

3. Choose the "Wix Members" app and add it to your site.

4. Customize your membership options, including free and paid plans, access to specific content, and user registration.

5. Set up member login and registration pages on your website.

6. Configure user profiles and access controls.

4. Forum or Community:

• To create a forum or community on your Wix website, you can use the "Wix Forum" app:

1. In the Wix Editor, click "Add" on the left sidebar.

2. Under "Apps," select "Community & Forums."

3. Choose the "Wix Forum" app and add it to your site.

4. Customize forum categories, topics, and user permissions.

5. Configure member profiles and interactions.

5. E-commerce and Online Store:

• For advanced e-commerce functionality, including product variations, inventory management, and payment processing, use the built-in Wix eCommerce features:

1. Add a Wix Online Store to your site, set up product listings, and configure payment and shipping options.

2. Customize the store design and layout to match your brand.

3. Implement marketing features like discounts, abandoned cart recovery, and product reviews.

6. Advanced SEO:

• Enhance your website's search engine optimization by utilizing advanced SEO tools and strategies, including optimizing meta tags, improving page speed, conducting competitive analysis, and tracking keyword rankings.

CHAPTER 5:

Mobile Optimization

Mobile optimization is crucial for ensuring that your website looks and functions well on smartphones and tablets. With an increasing number of users accessing websites on mobile devices, providing a mobile-friendly experience is essential. Here are key steps to optimize your website for mobile:

1. Choose a Mobile-Responsive Design:

• Start by selecting a mobile-responsive template or theme for your website. Most modern website builders, including Wix, offer mobile-responsive templates that adapt to different screen sizes automatically.

2. Prioritize Page Speed:

• Mobile users have less patience for slow-loading websites. Optimize your site's images, minimize code, and leverage browser caching to improve page load times. Tools like Google PageSpeed Insights can help identify performance issues.

3. Simplify Navigation:

• Streamline your site's navigation for mobile users. Use a clear and concise menu structure, and consider implementing a mobile-friendly hamburger menu (the three horizontal lines) for easier access to navigation links.

4. Responsive Design Elements:

• Ensure that all design elements, including images, buttons, and text, are responsive and adapt to different screen sizes. Test your website on various mobile devices to check for any layout issues.

5. Font Size and Readability:

• Use legible font sizes and ensure text is easy to read on smaller screens. Avoid using tiny fonts or overcrowding text on the screen.

6. Mobile-Friendly Forms:

• If your website includes forms for contact, registration, or purchases, optimize them for mobile. Use larger input fields and buttons for touchscreen convenience.

7. Touch-Friendly Buttons:

• Ensure that buttons and links are large enough and have enough spacing between them to accommodate touch interactions. This prevents accidental clicks and enhances the user experience.

8. Avoid Flash and Pop-Ups:

• Flash content doesn't work on most mobile devices, so avoid using it. Additionally, consider minimizing or eliminating pop-ups, as they can be intrusive on mobile screens.

9. Test Across Devices:

• Regularly test your website on various mobile devices and browsers to ensure compatibility and consistent performance.

10. Mobile SEO:

• Optimize your website for mobile SEO. This includes using mobile-friendly meta titles and descriptions, ensuring proper indexing, and adhering to Google's mobile-first indexing guidelines.

11. Accelerated Mobile Pages (AMP):

• Consider implementing AMP, a Google-backed project that provides a lightweight and fast-loading version of web pages, specifically designed for mobile users. AMP can help improve mobile search rankings.

12. Mobile-Friendly Content:

• Create content that is easy to consume on mobile devices. Use shorter paragraphs, concise headings, and avoid excessive use of images that may slow down page loading.

13. User Testing:

• Conduct user testing with real mobile users to gather feedback and identify any usability issues or areas for improvement.

14. Mobile Analytics:

• Use mobile analytics tools to track user behavior on your mobile site. This data can help you understand how users interact with your website on mobile devices and make informed optimization decisions.

Ensuring Your Website Is Mobile-Friendly

Ensuring your website is mobile-friendly is critical in today's digital landscape where a significant portion of internet traffic comes from mobile devices. Here are essential steps to make sure your website is mobile-friendly:

1. Use a Mobile-Responsive Design:

• Choose a website design or template that is mobile-responsive. Most modern website builders and content management systems (CMS) offer responsive themes that adapt to various screen sizes automatically.

2. Test on Multiple Devices:

• Regularly test your website on different mobile devices, such as smartphones and tablets, to ensure it appears and functions correctly on various screen sizes and operating systems.

3. Mobile-Friendly Navigation:

• Simplify your website's navigation for mobile users. Use a clear and concise menu structure, and consider implementing a mobile-friendly hamburger menu (the three horizontal lines) for easy access to navigation links.

4. Responsive Design Elements:

• Ensure that all design elements, including images, buttons, and text, are responsive and adjust to different screen sizes. Test your website to check for any layout or formatting issues on mobile devices.

5. Font Size and Readability:

• Use legible font sizes and ensure that text is easy to read on smaller screens. Avoid using tiny fonts or overcrowding text on the screen.

6. Touch-Friendly Buttons and Links:

• Make sure buttons and links are large enough and have sufficient spacing between them to accommodate touch interactions. This helps prevent accidental clicks and improves the user experience.

7. Optimize Images and Media:

• Compress and optimize images to reduce file sizes and improve page loading speed on mobile devices. Use responsive media elements that scale with the screen size.

8. Mobile-Friendly Forms:

• If your website includes forms for contact, registration, or purchases, optimize them for mobile. Use larger input fields and buttons for touchscreen convenience.

9. Avoid Flash and Pop-Ups:

• Flash content doesn't work on most mobile devices, so avoid using it. Additionally, consider minimizing or eliminating pop-ups, as they can be intrusive on mobile screens.

10. Mobile SEO:

vbnet

- Optimize your website for mobile SEO. This includes using mobile-friendly meta titles and descriptions, ensuring proper indexing, and adhering to Google's mobile-first indexing guidelines.

11. Accelerated Mobile Pages (AMP):

bash

- Consider implementing AMP, a Google-backed project that provides a lightweight and fast-loading version of web pages specifically designed for mobile users. AMP can help improve mobile search rankings.

12. Test on Mobile Emulators:

bash

- Use mobile emulator tools to simulate how your website appears and functions on various mobile devices. This can help identify and address issues before they affect real users.

13. User Testing:

sql

- Conduct user testing with real mobile users to gather feedback and identify any usability issues or areas for improvement.

14. Mobile Analytics:

vbnet

- Use mobile analytics tools to track user behavior on your mobile site. This data can help you understand how users interact with your website on mobile devices and make informed optimization decisions.

By following these steps and regularly maintaining your website's mobile-friendliness, you can provide an excellent user experience for mobile visitors and ensure that your website remains competitive in the mobile-driven digital landscape.

Adjusting The Mobile View In Wix Editor

Adjusting the mobile view in the Wix Editor allows you to fine-tune how your website appears and functions on mobile devices. Here's how you can adjust the mobile view in the Wix Editor:

1. Open Your Wix Website:

• Log in to your Wix account and open the website you want to edit.

2. Access the Wix Editor:

• Click on the "Edit Site" button to enter the Wix Editor for your website.

3. Select the Mobile View:

• In the top toolbar of the Wix Editor, you'll find options to switch between different views, including "Desktop," "Tablet," and "Mobile."

• Click on the "Mobile" view to switch to the mobile editing mode.

4. Adjust Layout and Design:

• In the mobile view, you can adjust various aspects of your website to optimize it for mobile devices. Here are some common adjustments you might make:

o Repositioning Elements: Drag and drop elements to reposition them on the mobile screen. You can rearrange sections, images, text, and more to ensure they display well on smaller screens.

o Resizing Elements: Resize elements by clicking and dragging their edges or corners. This helps you control the size and proportions of images, text boxes, buttons, and other content.

o Hiding or Showing Elements: Some elements that work well on desktop may not be necessary or suitable for mobile. You can hide or show specific elements in the mobile view by clicking the eye icon in the mobile editor.

o Font and Text Size: Adjust font sizes and spacing to ensure text is legible on mobile screens. Smaller screens may require larger font sizes for readability.

o **Menu and Navigation:** Modify your website's menu and navigation to make it more mobile-friendly. Consider using a mobile-responsive menu design, like a hamburger menu, for easier navigation.

5. Preview Your Changes:

• To see how your adjustments look on an actual mobile device, use the "Preview" button in the top toolbar. This allows you to view your website in a mobile preview mode.

6. Save Your Changes:

• Once you're satisfied with the adjustments you've made in the mobile view, be sure to click the "Save" button to save your changes.

7. Switch Back to Desktop View:

• You can switch back to the "Desktop" view or other device views at any time to make adjustments specific to those screen sizes.

8. Publish Your Site:

• After you've made all necessary adjustments and reviewed your mobile view, click the "Publish" button to make your changes live on the internet.

By adjusting the mobile view in the Wix Editor, you can ensure that your website provides a seamless and user-friendly experience for visitors using smartphones and tablets. Regularly reviewing and optimizing your mobile view is essential to keep up with changing design trends and user expectations.

CHAPTER 6:

Domain and Hosting

Understanding domains and hosting is essential when creating a website. These are fundamental components of how websites are identified and made accessible on the internet.

Domain:

A domain is the human-readable web address that people use to access your website. It serves as a unique identifier for your site on the internet. Here are some key points about domains:

1. Domain Name: A domain name consists of two main parts: the actual name (e.g., "example") and the domain extension (e.g., ".com"). Together, they form a complete web address, such as "example.com." You can choose a domain name that reflects your brand, business, or the content of your website.

2. Domain Registrar: To register a domain name, you'll need to use a domain registrar, which is a company that manages domain registrations. Popular domain registrars include GoDaddy, Namecheap, and Google Domains.

3. Domain Renewal: Domain names are usually registered on an annual basis, and you need to renew your registration to maintain ownership of the domain. Failure

to renew can result in losing your domain.

4. Domain Privacy: Domain registrars often offer domain privacy services to keep your personal information, such as your name and contact details, private in the domain's WHOIS database.

Hosting:

Web hosting refers to the service that stores your website's files, data, and content on a server and makes it accessible to users over the internet. Here are key points about web hosting:

1. Web Hosting Provider: A web hosting provider is a company that offers server space and services to host websites. Popular hosting providers include Bluehost, HostGator, SiteGround, and many others.

2. Types of Hosting: There are various types of web hosting, including:

o Shared Hosting: Multiple websites share resources on a single server, making it cost-effective for small websites.

o VPS Hosting: Virtual Private Server (VPS) hosting provides dedicated resources on a virtual server, offering more control and flexibility.

o Dedicated Hosting: With dedicated hosting, you have an entire server dedicated to your website, providing the highest level of performance and customization.

o Cloud Hosting: Cloud hosting uses a network of interconnected virtual servers to host websites, ensuring scalability and reliability.

3. Server Management: Depending on the hosting type, you may have different levels of control over the server. Shared hosting typically has limited control, while dedicated and

VPS hosting offer more customization options.

4. Technical Support: Hosting providers usually offer customer support to help with server-related issues, configuration, and troubleshooting.

5. Bandwidth and Storage: Hosting plans come with limitations on bandwidth (data transfer) and storage space. Choose a plan that suits your website's needs.

6. Server Location: The location of the server can impact website loading times for visitors. Choose a hosting provider with server locations that align with your target audience's location.

Domain and Hosting Relationship:

To have a functional website, you typically need both a domain and hosting:

• Domain Pointer: Your domain serves as a pointer to your hosting server. When someone enters your domain in a web browser, it directs them to the server where your website's files are stored.

• Email Hosting: In addition to hosting a website, many hosting providers offer email hosting services, allowing you to create custom email addresses associated with your domain (e.g., info@example.com).

Understanding the roles of domains and hosting is essential when setting up and maintaining a website. You need a domain to provide a recognizable web address, and hosting to store and serve the website's content to visitors on the internet.

Registering A Custom Domain Through Wix

Registering a custom domain through Wix is a straightforward process that allows you to use a unique web address for your Wix website. Here's how to register a custom domain through Wix:

1. Sign in to Your Wix Account:

• Ensure that you're logged in to your Wix account.

2. Access the Wix Editor:

• From your Wix dashboard, click on the website you want to connect a custom domain to. This will open the Wix Editor for your website.

3. Choose "Connect Domain":

• In the Wix Editor, go to the top left corner, and click on the "Connect Domain" button. This button may also appear as "Get a Domain" or "Add a Domain" depending on your current setup.

4. Select "Buy a New Domain":

• If you don't already own a domain, choose the option to "Buy a New Domain." If you already own a domain and want to connect it to your Wix website, select the option to "Connect a Domain You Already Own."

5. Search for Your Domain:

• If you're buying a new domain, you'll be prompted to search for an available domain name. Enter your desired domain name (e.g., "mywebsite.com") and click "Search."

6. Choose Your Domain:

• Wix will display a list of available domains that match your search. Select the domain you want to purchase from the list.

7. Review and Confirm:

• Review the domain you've chosen, its availability, and the associated cost. If you're satisfied, click "Continue."

8. Create or Sign In to Your Wix Account:

• If you're not already signed in to your Wix account, you'll be prompted to either sign in or create a new account. Follow the prompts to complete this step.

9. Complete the Purchase:

• Enter your billing and payment information to complete the purchase of the domain. Wix will guide you through the payment process.

10. Verify Ownership:

vbnet

- After purchasing the domain, you may need to verify your ownership. Wix will provide instructions on how to do this, which typically involves confirming your email address.

11. Connect the Domain:

vbnet

- Once you've completed the purchase and ownership verification, Wix will guide you through the process of connecting the domain to your Wix website. This may involve updating DNS settings or configuring the domain settings.

12. Wait for DNS Propagation:

vbnet

- It can take up to 48 hours for DNS changes to propagate across the internet. During this time, your custom domain will become accessible to visitors.

13. Confirm Domain Connection:

vbnet

- After DNS propagation is complete, confirm that your custom domain is correctly connected to your Wix website by visiting your website using the custom domain (e.g., www.yourdomain.com).

By following these steps, you'll successfully register a custom domain through Wix and connect it to your website, giving your site a professional and unique web address.

Connecting An Existing Domain To Your Wix Site

Connecting an existing domain to your Wix site is a process that allows you to use your own domain name (which you've previously registered with a domain registrar) with your Wix website. Here's a step-by-step guide on how to connect an existing domain to your Wix site:

1. Sign in to Your Wix Account:

• Ensure that you are signed in to your Wix account.

2. Access the Wix Editor:

• From your Wix dashboard, click on the website you want to connect your existing domain to. This will open the Wix Editor for your website.

3. Go to "Settings":

• In the Wix Editor, click on the "Settings" option in the left-hand sidebar.

4. Select "Domains":

• In the "Settings" menu, select the "Domains" option.

5. Click on "Connect a Domain You Already Own":

• Under the "Connect a Domain" section, click on "Connect a Domain You Already Own." If you've already connected a domain, you'll see the option to "Change Domain."

6. Enter Your Existing Domain:

• In the next screen, enter the domain name you want to connect to your Wix website (e.g., www.yourdomain.com). Then click the "Next" button.

7. Confirm Ownership:

• Wix will prompt you to verify your ownership of the domain. You can choose one of the following verification methods:

o Add a TXT Record: You'll be provided with specific DNS settings (TXT records) to add to your domain's DNS configuration with your domain registrar.

o Update Name Servers: Wix will provide you with new name server (NS) records to replace the ones currently set with your domain registrar.

8. Update DNS Settings:

• Depending on the verification method you selected, follow the instructions to either add the provided TXT records or update your domain's name servers. You'll need to do this with your domain registrar (the company where you registered your domain).

9. Verify Domain Connection:

• Once you've updated your DNS settings or name servers, return to the Wix domain settings and click the "Verify Connection" button.

10. Wait for DNS Propagation:

vbnet

- It can take up to 48 hours for DNS changes to propagate across the internet. During this time, your existing domain will become accessible with your Wix website.

11. Confirm Domain Connection:

vbnet

- After DNS propagation is complete, confirm that your existing domain is correctly connected to your Wix website by visiting your website using the existing domain (e.g., www.yourdomain.com).

By following these steps and ensuring proper DNS configuration with your domain registrar, you can successfully connect an existing domain to your Wix website. This allows you to use your own domain name while enjoying the benefits of Wix's website building and hosting services.

Managing Hosting And Domain Settings

Managing hosting and domain settings involves various tasks related to the configuration, maintenance, and customization of your website's hosting and domain services. Here are steps and considerations for managing these settings:

1. Accessing Hosting and Domain Control Panels:

• Depending on your hosting provider and domain registrar, you'll have control panels or dashboards where you can manage settings. Log in to your hosting and domain accounts to access these panels.

2. Updating DNS Records:

• DNS (Domain Name System) records control how domain names are mapped to IP addresses. You can update DNS records to:

o Point Your Domain: Configure DNS records to point your domain to the correct hosting server's IP address.

o Set Up Subdomains: Create subdomains (e.g., blog.yourdomain.com) by adding appropriate DNS records.

o Configure Email Settings: Set up email services associated with your domain.

3. Changing Name Servers:

• If you want to use a different hosting provider, you may need to change your domain's name servers to those provided by the new hosting company. This directs traffic to the correct server.

4. Domain Privacy Protection:

• Most domain registrars offer domain privacy services that protect your personal information in the WHOIS database. You can enable or disable this service.

5. Domain Renewal:

• Ensure your domain registration is up to date by renewing it before it expires. Many registrars offer automatic renewal options.

6. SSL Certificates:

• If your website handles sensitive information or requires user logins, consider installing an SSL certificate. This secures data transmission between your website and visitors. Some hosting providers offer free SSL certificates.

7. Email Configuration:

• If you use email associated with your domain (e.g., info@yourdomain.com), configure email settings through your hosting or domain control panel. Set up email accounts, forwarding, and other email-related features.

8. Hosting Features:

• Explore and configure hosting features offered by your hosting provider, such as:

o Database Management: Create and manage databases for your website's content and applications.

o File Management: Upload and manage website files through FTP or a file manager.

o Backup and Restore: Regularly back up your website data and configure automated backup options.

o Security: Set up security measures, like firewalls and malware scanning, to protect your website.

9. Website Maintenance:

• Regularly update your website's content, themes, plugins, and software to ensure security and functionality. Check for software updates in your hosting control panel.

10. Traffic and Analytics:

vbnet

- Monitor website traffic and performance through

analytics tools provided by your hosting provider or third-party services like Google Analytics.

11. Technical Support:

vbnet

- Reach out to your hosting provider or domain registrar's technical support if you encounter technical issues or need assistance with settings. Most providers offer support through email, live chat, or phone.

12. Domain Transfers and Renewals:

vbnet

- If you're changing domain registrars or hosting providers, follow the specific transfer procedures provided by both parties. Ensure your domain registration remains valid throughout the process.

13. DNSSEC (DNS Security Extensions):

bash

- Consider enabling DNSSEC for added security, which helps prevent DNS spoofing and tampering.

14. Manage Subdomains:

rust

- If you use subdomains (e.g., blog.yourdomain.com), configure and manage them according to your website's needs.

Managing hosting and domain settings requires careful attention to detail to ensure your website remains accessible, secure, and functional. Be sure to document any changes you make to your settings for future reference.

CHAPTER 7:

Launching Your Website

Launching your website using Wix is a straightforward process. Wix provides user-friendly tools and features to help you prepare your website for launch and make it accessible to the public. Here's a step-by-step guide to launch your website on Wix:

1. Finalize Your Website:

• Before launching, ensure that your website is complete and thoroughly tested. Review all pages, content, links, and functionality to make sure everything is working as expected.

2. Upgrade to a Premium Plan (if necessary):

• Depending on your needs, you might want to consider upgrading to a premium plan if you haven't already. Wix offers various premium plans with additional features and benefits.

3. Connect a Custom Domain (if applicable):

• If you have a custom domain (e.g., www.yourdomain.com), make sure it is properly connected to your Wix website. You can do this by going to Wix's domain settings and following the steps for connecting an existing domain.

4. Configure SEO Settings:

• Optimize your website's SEO settings, including meta titles, descriptions, and keywords. This will help improve your website's visibility in search engines.

5. Set Up Google Analytics:

• Consider integrating Google Analytics with your Wix website to track visitor data, traffic sources, and other valuable insights.

6. Mobile Optimization:

• Ensure that your website is mobile-responsive and looks good on various devices, including smartphones and tablets.

7. Test Your Website:

• Test your website thoroughly on different browsers and devices to catch any last-minute issues.

8. Backup Your Website:

• Create a backup of your website, especially if you plan to make significant changes or updates in the future.

9. Prepare a Launch Announcement:

• If you want to build anticipation, create a launch announcement or promotional content to let your audience know about your website's upcoming launch date.

10. Make Any Necessary Content Updates:

sql

- Double-check all content, images, and links to ensure they are up-to-date and accurate.

11. Privacy Policy and Legal Documents:

css

- If applicable, add a privacy policy, terms of service, or any other necessary legal documents to your website.

12. Launch Your Website:

vbnet

- When you're ready to launch, follow these steps:

  - In the Wix Editor, click "Publish" or "Publish Now."

  - If prompted, select your desired domain (if you have multiple domains connected).

  - Click "Publish" to make your website live.

13. Promote Your Launch:

vbnet

- After your website is live, promote its launch through social media, email newsletters, and other marketing channels to drive traffic and engagement.

14. Monitor and Maintain:

vbnet

- Continuously monitor your website's performance, user feedback, and analytics. Make updates and improvements as needed to enhance the user experience.

Remember that launching your website is just the beginning. Regularly update your content, engage with your audience, and refine your website to meet your goals and objectives. Wix provides tools and resources to help you manage and grow your online presence effectively.

Pre-launch checklist

A pre-launch checklist is essential to ensure that your website is fully prepared for its debut. Here's a comprehensive checklist to follow before launching your website:

1. Content Review:

• ✔ Proofread all content for spelling and grammatical errors.

• ✔ Verify that all text is accurate and up-to-date.

• ✔ Confirm that images and multimedia assets are optimized and relevant.

• ✔ Check for broken links and ensure that all internal and external links work correctly.

2. Design and Layout:

• ✔ Review the overall design and layout of your website for consistency and aesthetics.

• ✔ Ensure that your website is mobile-responsive and looks good on various devices.

• ✔ Test different browsers to confirm compatibility.

3. Functionality:

• ✔ Verify that all interactive elements, such as forms, buttons, and navigation, work as intended.

• ✔ Test any e-commerce or payment functionalities for smooth transactions.

• ✔ Ensure that any multimedia, such as videos and audio, plays without issues.

4. SEO and Metadata:

• ✔ Optimize SEO settings, including meta titles, descriptions, and keywords.

• ✔ Check that URLs are descriptive and contain relevant keywords.

• ✓ Ensure that images have alt tags for accessibility and SEO.

5. Security:

• ✓ Implement security measures, such as SSL certificates if you collect sensitive data.

• ✓ Set up security plugins or measures to protect against malware and hacking attempts.

6. Performance:

• ✓ Test page loading speed and optimize images and code as needed.

• ✓ Enable browser caching to improve performance.

• ✓ Check for any 404 error pages and redirect them to relevant content.

7. Mobile Optimization:

• ✓ Confirm that your website is fully functional and user-friendly on mobile devices.

• ✓ Test navigation, buttons, and text readability on smartphones and tablets.

8. Analytics and Tracking:

• ✓ Set up Google Analytics or other tracking tools to monitor website traffic.

• ✓ Ensure that tracking codes are correctly implemented on all pages.

9. Forms and Contact Information:

• ✓ Test contact forms and ensure they deliver submissions to the correct email addresses.

• ✓ Provide accurate and up-to-date contact information.

10. Legal Compliance:

csharp

- ✓ Include necessary legal documents, such as a privacy policy and terms of service.

- ✓ Ensure compliance with GDPR or other relevant data protection regulations.

11. Backup:

vbnet

- ✓ Create a backup of your website's files and database before launch.

12. Testing:

sql

- ✓ Conduct user testing with a diverse group of users to gather feedback.

- ✓ Check for 404 errors, broken links, or missing pages.

13. Domain and Hosting:

vbnet

- ✓ Ensure that your custom domain is correctly connected to your hosting.

- ✓ Verify that hosting settings are optimized for performance and security.

14. Social Sharing and Open Graph:

vbnet

- ✓ Set up social sharing metadata to control how your website appears on social media.

- ✓ Test social sharing functionality to confirm that shared links display correctly.

15. Launch Announcement:

css

- ✔ Plan and schedule a launch announcement or promotional content to inform your audience about your website's launch date.

16. Review and Approvals:

arduino

- ✔ Have your team or stakeholders review the website for final approval.

- ✔ Make any necessary revisions based on feedback.

17. Emergency Plan:

csharp

- ✔ Have a plan in place for dealing with unexpected issues or downtime during the launch.

18. Publishing and Backup:

arduino

- ✔ Publish your website using your hosting platform's publishing tools.

- ✔ Create a backup of your website after the final review and approval.

19. Monitor and Adjust:

vbnet

- ✔ Continuously monitor your website's performance and user feedback after launch.

- ✔ Be prepared to make updates and improvements as needed.

By following this pre-launch checklist, you can ensure

that your website is in optimal condition and ready to impress visitors when it goes live. Regular maintenance and updates will help you maintain a successful online presence.

Afterall, make it known to your audience

Announcing your website to your audience is a crucial step to drive traffic, engagement, and awareness. It's essential to create a compelling and well-executed announcement plan to make a strong impact. Here's a step-by-step guide to announcing your website effectively:

1. Define Your Target Audience:

• Determine who your primary audience is and what their interests, preferences, and needs are. Tailor your announcement to resonate with this specific group.

2. Craft a Compelling Message:

• Create a clear and concise message that communicates the value and purpose of your website. Highlight what visitors can expect to find and why they should explore it.

3. Utilize Multiple Channels:

• Spread the word through various communication channels to reach a wider audience. Consider using the following platforms:

o Social Media: Share announcement posts on your social media profiles, including Facebook, Twitter, Instagram, LinkedIn, and any other relevant platforms.

o Email: Send an email announcement to your subscribers

or mailing list. Craft a personalized and engaging email message.

o Website Blog: Write a blog post on your website to introduce and explain the new website.

o Press Release: If your website launch is significant, consider creating a press release to distribute to media outlets.

o Forums and Communities: Share your announcement on relevant online forums and communities where your target audience participates.

o Newsletters: If you have partnerships or affiliations, consider including your website announcement in their newsletters.

o Offline Marketing: Depending on your audience, you might consider print media, direct mail, or events.

o Paid Advertising: If you have the budget, invest in paid advertising on platforms like Google Ads, Facebook Ads, or LinkedIn Ads to promote your website.

4. Create Engaging Content:

• Use eye-catching visuals, videos, or infographics to make your announcement more engaging and shareable.

• Craft a compelling headline and call-to-action (CTA) to encourage users to visit your website.

5. Leverage Influencers and Partnerships:

• Collaborate with influencers or partners who have a relevant audience. They can help amplify your announcement through their own networks.

6. Schedule Your Announcement:

• Choose a strategic time and date for your announcement

to maximize visibility and engagement. Consider factors like your audience's online activity and time zones.

7. Monitor and Respond:

• Be prepared to monitor the response to your announcement across different channels. Respond promptly to comments, questions, and feedback.

8. Measure Your Success:

• Use analytics tools to track the performance of your announcement. Measure website traffic, engagement metrics, and conversion rates to gauge the impact.

9. Follow-Up Engagement:

• Keep your audience engaged after the initial announcement. Regularly share new content, updates, and promotions to maintain interest.

10. Gather Feedback:

vbnet

- Encourage users to provide feedback on your website's usability, content, and functionality. Use this feedback to make improvements.

11. Social Sharing:

vbnet

- Include social sharing buttons on your website to make it easy for visitors to share your content and announcements with their networks.

12. Consistency:

css

- Maintain a consistent brand voice and messaging across all channels to reinforce your website's identity.

13. Adapt and Refine:

csharp

- Continuously analyze your announcement strategy and make adjustments based on what works best for your audience.

Announcing your website to your audience is not a one-time event. It's an ongoing process of building and maintaining engagement with your target audience. By carefully planning and executing your announcement, you can create a strong initial impact and set the stage for long-term success.

Strategies for driving traffic

Driving initial traffic to your website is a crucial step in gaining visibility, building your audience, and achieving your online goals. Here are some effective strategies to attract that initial surge of visitors:

1. Search Engine Optimization (SEO):

• Optimize your website's content for search engines. Research and use relevant keywords, optimize meta tags, and ensure your content is high-quality and informative. SEO helps your website rank higher in search engine results pages (SERPs), increasing organic traffic.

2. Social Media Promotion:

• Leverage your social media platforms to promote your website. Share links to your website's pages, blog posts, or products. Create engaging content and use relevant hashtags to reach a broader audience.

3. Email Marketing:

• Use your existing email list to send out announcements

about your website launch. Encourage your subscribers to visit and explore your new site. Craft a compelling email message with clear CTAs.

4. Content Marketing:

• Create valuable and shareable content, such as blog posts, articles, infographics, videos, or podcasts. Share this content on your website and through social media. Quality content can attract and retain visitors.

5. Pay-Per-Click (PPC) Advertising:

• Consider running PPC advertising campaigns on platforms like Google Ads or social media platforms. Set a budget and target specific keywords or demographics to drive traffic to your website.

6. Guest Blogging:

• Write guest posts for reputable websites and include a link back to your site in your author bio or within the content. This can help you tap into established audiences and drive targeted traffic.

7. Influencer Marketing:

• Collaborate with influencers in your niche who have a significant following. They can promote your website to their audience through sponsored content, reviews, or mentions.

8. Online Communities and Forums:

• Participate in relevant online communities and forums related to your industry or niche. Provide helpful answers, insights, and solutions while subtly promoting your website when appropriate.

9. Social Bookmarking and Content Sharing Sites:

• Share your website's content on social bookmarking sites like Reddit, Pinterest, or Digg. These platforms can generate substantial traffic if your content resonates with users.

10. Podcasts and Webinars:

css

- Host or participate in podcasts or webinars related to your niche. Mention your website and provide links in your podcast episodes or webinar presentations.

11. Cross-Promotion:

python

- Partner with other websites, businesses, or influencers for cross-promotion. Promote each other's content or products to access each other's audiences.

12. Online Advertising:

sql

- Invest in online advertising through platforms like Facebook, Instagram, or LinkedIn to target specific demographics and interests.

13. Quora and Q&A Sites:

vbnet

- Answer questions on Q&A platforms like Quora, Yahoo Answers, or Stack Exchange. Provide valuable answers and link to your website when relevant.

14. Press Releases:

arduino

- Write and distribute a press release about your website launch. Send it to relevant media outlets and industry publications.

15. Referral Traffic:

vbnet

- Build relationships with other websites and request backlinks to your site. High-quality backlinks can significantly boost your website's visibility.

16. Online Directories:

vbnet

- Submit your website to relevant online directories and listings, such as Google My Business, Yelp, or industry-specific directories.

17. Engage with Your Audience:

vbnet

- Encourage engagement on your website through comments, social sharing, and discussions. An engaged audience is more likely to return and refer others.

18. Monitor and Analyze:

vbnet

- Use web analytics tools like Google Analytics to monitor your website's traffic sources, user behavior, and conversion rates. Adjust your strategies based on data insights.

Remember that driving initial traffic is just the beginning. Focus on providing valuable content and a positive user experience to retain visitors and encourage them to return to your website. Building a consistent flow of traffic takes time, so be patient and persistent in your efforts.

CHAPTER 8:

*Maintaining and Growing
Your Website*

Regular Website Maintenance Tasks

Growing and maintaining your website is an ongoing process that involves regular tasks to ensure it remains up-to-date, secure, and optimized for your audience. Here's a list of essential tasks for website growth and maintenance:

1. Content Updates:

• Regularly update your website with fresh and relevant content. Publish new blog posts, articles, or products to keep your audience engaged and attract new visitors.

2. Security Updates:

• Keep your website's software, themes, plugins, and scripts up-to-date to protect against security vulnerabilities. Regularly apply updates and security patches.

3. Backup Your Website:

• Schedule automated backups of your website's files and database. Ensure backups are stored securely off-site so that you can restore your site in case of data loss or security issues.

4. Monitor Website Speed:

• Regularly test your website's loading speed and performance. Optimize images, use caching, and minimize code to improve speed.

5. SEO Maintenance:

• Continuously optimize your website for search engines. Update metadata, refresh keywords, and review your site's structure for SEO improvements.

6. Review and Remove Broken Links:

• Periodically check for broken links on your website and fix or remove them to maintain a good user experience and SEO.

7. Analyze Website Traffic:

• Use analytics tools to monitor website traffic, user behavior, and conversion rates. Analyze data to identify trends and areas for improvement.

8. Mobile Optimization:

• Ensure your website is fully optimized for mobile devices. Test on various screen sizes and devices to maintain a positive mobile user experience.

9. User Feedback:

• Encourage users to provide feedback on your website's usability, content, and features. Use this feedback to make improvements.

10. Website Security:

rust

- Regularly scan your website for malware and vulnerabilities. Consider implementing a web application firewall (WAF) for added protection.

11. Content Promotion:

vbnet

- Continuously promote your website's content through social media, email newsletters, and other marketing channels to attract new visitors.

12. User Engagement:

csharp

- Engage with your audience through comments, forums, and social media. Encourage discussions and build a community around your website.

13. Monitor Comments and Spam:

css

- Moderate comments and user-generated content to prevent spam and maintain a positive online environment.

14. Update Legal Documents:

vbnet

- Review and update privacy policies, terms of service, and other legal documents as needed to comply with changing regulations.

15. A/B Testing:

vbnet

- Experiment with A/B testing to optimize elements of your website, such as headlines, call-to-action buttons, and landing pages, for better conversion rates.

16. Regular Backups:

vbnet

- Verify that your backup system is working correctly by periodically restoring from backups to ensure data integrity.

17. 404 Error Monitoring:

vbnet

- Set up 404 error monitoring to identify and fix broken links or missing pages promptly.

18. Accessibility:

python

- Ensure your website is accessible to all users, including those with disabilities. Regularly test for accessibility compliance.

19. Server and Hosting Review:

vbnet

- Evaluate your hosting plan's performance, scalability, and security. Consider upgrading or changing hosts if necessary.

20. Content Calendar:

css

- Create and follow a content calendar to plan and schedule content updates, ensuring consistency and alignment with your goals.

21. User Experience (UX) Enhancements:

kotlin

- Continually improve the user experience by simplifying navigation, improving site structure, and enhancing user interface elements.

22. Check for Outdated Information:

KALARA KORU

- Verify that your backup system is working correctly by periodically restoring from backups to ensure data integrity.

17. 404 Error Monitoring:

vbnet

- Set up 404 error monitoring to identify and fix broken links or missing pages promptly.

18. Accessibility:

python

- Ensure your website is accessible to all users, including those with disabilities. Regularly test for accessibility compliance.

19. Server and Hosting Review:

vbnet

- Evaluate your hosting plan's performance, scalability, and security. Consider upgrading or changing hosts if necessary.

20. Content Calendar:

css

- Create and follow a content calendar to plan and schedule content updates, ensuring consistency and alignment with your goals.

21. User Experience (UX) Enhancements:

kotlin

- Continually improve the user experience by simplifying navigation, improving site structure, and enhancing user interface elements.

22. Check for Outdated Information:

rust

- Regularly review your website for outdated information, such as contact details, product descriptions, or pricing.

23. Monitor for Downtime:

vbnet

- Use website monitoring services to receive alerts if your site experiences downtime. Take immediate action if any issues arise.

24. Legal Compliance:

vbnet

- Stay informed about legal requirements related to your website, such as GDPR or CCPA, and ensure compliance.

25. Social Media Integration:

arduino

- Integrate your website with social media profiles and maintain a consistent online presence across platforms.

By regularly performing these maintenance tasks, you'll keep your website running smoothly, improve its performance, and continue to attract and engage your audience as your online presence grows.

Monitoring Website Performance

Monitoring website performance is crucial to ensure your site operates smoothly, loads quickly, and provides an excellent user experience. Monitoring your website's performance is an ongoing task that requires regular attention and proactive measures. By regularly analyzing key performance indicators and addressing issues promptly, you can maintain a high-performing website that provides an excellent user experience and supports your online goals.

1. Use Website Performance Tools:

• Utilize website performance monitoring tools and services such as Google PageSpeed Insights, GTmetrix, Pingdom, or WebPageTest. These tools provide insights into various aspects of your website's performance.

2. Test Page Load Speed:

• Regularly test the loading speed of your website's pages. Faster loading times improve user experience and SEO rankings. Aim for a load time of under three seconds.

3. Monitor Uptime:

• Use website monitoring services or tools to check your site's uptime and receive alerts if your site goes down. Downtime can harm your reputation and lead to lost visitors.

4. Track Page Errors:

• Set up error tracking to monitor for 404 (page not found) errors and other server errors. Fix errors promptly to improve user experience and SEO.

5. Check Mobile Responsiveness:

• Ensure your website is mobile-responsive by testing it on various devices and screen sizes. Tools like Google's Mobile-Friendly Test can help.

6. Analyze Page Speed Metrics:

• Examine specific metrics like First Contentful Paint (FCP), Largest Contentful Paint (LCP), and Cumulative Layout

Shift (CLS) to identify areas for improvement in page rendering.

7. Monitor Website Traffic:

• Use web analytics tools such as Google Analytics to track website traffic, user behavior, and engagement metrics. Regularly review these insights to make informed decisions.

8. Assess Server Performance:

• Evaluate your web hosting server's performance by monitoring CPU usage, memory, and response times. Consider upgrading your hosting plan if needed.

9. Content Delivery Network (CDN) Performance:

• If you use a CDN to serve website assets, monitor its performance and ensure it effectively caches and delivers content to users worldwide.

10. Browser Compatibility:

vbnet

- Test your website on various web browsers (Chrome, Firefox, Safari, Edge, etc.) to ensure compatibility and consistent rendering.

11. Security Monitoring:

css

- Regularly scan your website for security vulnerabilities and malware. Use security plugins or services to help protect your site from threats.

12. SEO Performance:

vbnet

- Keep an eye on your website's SEO performance

by monitoring keyword rankings, organic traffic, and backlinks. Adjust your SEO strategy accordingly.

13. User Experience (UX) Testing:

sql

- Conduct usability tests and gather feedback from users to identify areas where the user experience can be improved.

14. Content Management:

vbnet

- Ensure that your content management system (CMS) and plugins are up-to-date, as outdated software can lead to performance issues and security vulnerabilities.

15. Regular Audits:

vbnet

- Perform regular website audits to identify and fix issues related to site structure, internal linking, and metadata.

16. Mobile App Performance (if applicable):

vbnet

- If you have a mobile app associated with your website, monitor its performance, and ensure it aligns with your website's goals.

17. Content Performance:

css

- Analyze the performance of individual pieces of content (e.g., blog posts, product pages) to identify high-performing and underperforming content. Make updates as needed.

18. Regularly Review and Adjust:

rust

- Set up a schedule for reviewing performance metrics and make adjustments based on your findings. Continuously optimize your website for better performance.

Expanding Your Website's Features And Content

Expanding your website's features and content is essential for keeping your audience engaged, attracting new visitors, and achieving your online goals. Expanding your website's features and content is an ongoing process that requires dedication and strategic planning. By consistently delivering value to your audience, staying adaptable, and refining your strategies based on feedback and analytics, you can successfully grow and maintain a thriving online presence.

1. Content Strategy:

• Develop a clear content strategy that aligns with your website's goals and audience. Consider the type of content you want to create, how often you'll publish, and the topics you'll cover.

2. Create High-Quality Content:

• Focus on creating informative, valuable, and well-researched content that addresses the needs and interests of your target audience. Consistently publish blog posts, articles, videos, infographics, and other relevant content.

3. Keyword Research:

• Perform keyword research to identify the topics and keywords your audience is searching for. Use SEO tools to find relevant keywords and incorporate them naturally into your content.

4. Content Calendar:

• Create a content calendar to plan and schedule content creation. A calendar helps you stay organized and ensures a consistent publishing schedule.

5. Engage with Your Audience:

• Encourage audience engagement through comments, social media, and forums. Respond to comments and interact with your community to build a loyal following.

6. Diversify Content Formats:

• Experiment with different content formats to appeal to a broader audience. Consider using podcasts, webinars, quizzes, and interactive content.

7. Expand Your Product or Service Offerings:

• If you offer products or services, consider expanding your offerings to meet customer needs. Launch new products, services, or variations based on market demand.

8. Implement Advanced Features:

• Integrate advanced features like e-commerce, memberships, booking systems, and community forums to enhance user experience and offer more value.

9. User-Generated Content:

• Encourage user-generated content, such as reviews, testimonials, and user-generated articles. This can boost engagement and provide social proof.

10. Collaborate and Guest Post:

vbnet

- Collaborate with influencers, experts, or other websites in your niche. Guest posting and collaborations can introduce your website to new audiences.

11. Localize Content (if applicable):

css

- If your target audience is global, consider localizing content to reach international markets. Translate content and adapt it to regional preferences and trends.

12. Monitor Analytics:

css

- Regularly review website analytics to identify which content performs well and which needs improvement. Use data to guide your content strategy.

13. Social Media Integration:

css

- Share your website content on social media platforms to reach a wider audience. Use social media management tools to schedule posts and analyze performance.

14. Email Marketing:

css

- Use email marketing campaigns to promote new content, products, or services to your subscribers. Encourage users to sign up for newsletters to stay updated.

15. Test and Optimize:

css

- Continually test different content and features to see what resonates best with your audience. Use A/B testing to refine elements like headlines, calls-to-action, and landing pages.

16. User Experience (UX) Improvements:

vbnet

- Regularly assess and enhance your website's user experience. Ensure that navigation is intuitive, pages load quickly, and the design remains visually appealing.

17. Stay Informed:

vbnet

- Keep up with industry trends and changes in your niche to stay relevant. Attend webinars, conferences, and workshops to expand your knowledge.

18. Encourage Feedback:

rust

- Ask for feedback from your audience and incorporate their suggestions for improvement. Conduct surveys or use feedback forms.

19. Plan for Scalability:

vbnet

- As you expand, plan for scalability by ensuring that your website can handle increased traffic and features without compromising performance.

20. Set Clear Goals:

rust

- Define specific goals for your website expansion efforts, such as increasing traffic, boosting sales, or growing your email list. Regularly assess progress toward these goals.

Engaging with your audience through blogs and social media

Engaging with your audience through blogs and social media is a powerful way to build a loyal community, foster relationships, and drive traffic to your website. Engaging with your audience through blogs and social media requires ongoing effort and genuine interaction. It's about building a community around your brand, fostering trust, and providing value. By consistently creating quality content and actively participating in conversations, you can strengthen your online presence and connect with your audience on a deeper level.

Engaging Through Blogs:

1. Understand Your Audience:

o Know your target audience's interests, needs, and pain points. Tailor your blog content to address these.

2. Create Valuable Content:

o Publish high-quality, informative, and engaging blog posts that provide solutions, insights, or entertainment to your audience.

3. Consistency is Key:

o Establish a regular posting schedule to keep your audience engaged. Consistency builds trust and encourages return visits.

4. Encourage Comments:

o Invite readers to leave comments and ask questions at the end of your blog posts. Respond to comments promptly to foster discussions.

5. Share Personal Stories:

o Share personal anecdotes or experiences related to your niche or industry. Personal stories can make your blog more relatable and memorable.

6. Use Visuals:

o Incorporate images, infographics, and videos to make your content more engaging and shareable.

7. Incorporate CTAs:

o Include clear and compelling calls-to-action (CTAs) within your blog posts to encourage readers to take the next step, such as subscribing to your newsletter or exploring related content.

8. Promote Sharing:

o Add social sharing buttons to your blog posts to make it easy for readers to share your content with their networks.

9. Offer Freebies or Resources:

o Provide downloadable resources, such as ebooks, templates, or checklists, to incentivize email sign-ups and engagement.

Engaging Through Social Media:

1. Choose the Right Platforms:

o Identify the social media platforms where your target audience is most active. Focus your efforts on those platforms.

2. Consistent Branding:

o Maintain a consistent brand identity, including your profile picture, cover photo, and bio, across all social media profiles.

3. Content Variety:

o Share a mix of content types, including blog posts, videos, images, polls, and user-generated content, to keep your feed interesting.

4. Interact Actively:

o Respond to comments, mentions, and direct messages in a timely and friendly manner. Engage in conversations with your audience.

5. Use Hashtags Strategically:

o Incorporate relevant hashtags to increase the discoverability of your content. Research popular hashtags in your niche.

6. Host Q&A Sessions:

o Conduct live Q&A sessions or AMAs (Ask Me Anything) on platforms like Instagram, Facebook Live, or Twitter to directly engage with your audience.

7. Contests and Giveaways:

o Host contests, giveaways, or challenges to encourage user participation and create excitement around your brand.

8. Share User-Generated Content:

o Showcase content created by your audience (with permission), such as testimonials, reviews, or photos using your products or services.

9. Provide Value:

o Share informative, entertaining, or inspirational content

that resonates with your audience's interests and needs.

10. Monitor Analytics:

o Use social media analytics tools to track engagement metrics, such as likes, shares, and comments. Adjust your strategy based on performance data.

11. Adapt to Trends:

o Stay updated with social media trends and incorporate them into your content strategy when relevant.

12. Be Authentic:

o Show the human side of your brand by sharing behind-the-scenes glimpses, team stories, and candid moments.

13. Social Listening:

o Pay attention to discussions and mentions related to your niche or industry. Engage in relevant conversations and provide valuable insights.

CONCLUSION

In conclusion, this book has served as a comprehensive guide to mastering the art of website creation using Wix. Throughout the chapters, we've explored the ins and outs of this versatile website builder, empowering you with the knowledge and skills needed to craft a stunning online presence. As we wrap up our journey, let's take a moment to recap some key takeaways from our exploration.

First and foremost, we've learned that creating a website with Wix is not just about crafting a digital space; it's about bringing your vision to life. From the initial steps of setting up your Wix account to navigating the intricacies of the Wix Editor and choosing the right plan, you've acquired the tools necessary to lay a strong foundation for your online venture.

One of the most critical aspects we've emphasized is the importance of defining clear goals and objectives for your website. Understanding your purpose and audience is the compass that guides your content, design, and overall strategy. By setting well-defined goals, you've paved the way for a purpose-driven online presence.

Our journey through the Wix Editor interface has given you the ability to customize your website's layout, colors, fonts, and pages. You've delved into the world of SEO, mastering the art of optimizing your site to be more discoverable by search engines. With a focus on creating compelling, SEO-friendly content, you've learned how to not only attract visitors but also engage them effectively.

We've also explored advanced features like integrating third-party apps, setting up e-commerce capabilities, and implementing memberships, all of which have expanded your website's potential. We've emphasized the importance of mobile optimization, ensuring that your site is not just visually appealing but also fully functional on all devices.

As we conclude, remember that the journey of website ownership is an ongoing one. Websites are dynamic entities that require continuous attention and improvement. Encourage yourself to stay curious, to adapt to evolving trends, and to seek out opportunities for growth. The digital landscape is ever-changing, and your website should evolve along with it.

Lastly, let's reflect on the power of Wix for website creation. This platform has demonstrated its versatility, user-friendliness, and capability to bring your vision to life. Whether you're a seasoned website owner or just starting your online journey, Wix provides the tools and resources to help you succeed.

In the age of the internet, your website is your digital storefront, your portfolio, your voice, and your connection to the world. It has the potential to be a powerful tool for personal expression, business growth, or community building. Embrace the possibilities, and remember that with dedication and the knowledge you've gained from this guide, the sky's the limit in the world of website creation.

So, as you embark on or continue your journey as a website owner, may you be inspired to continually improve your online presence, tell your unique story, and make your mark on the digital landscape. Your website is a canvas waiting for your creative touch, and with Wix as your trusted companion, the future of your online journey is boundless. Happy website building, and may your online endeavors be a resounding success!